Ь ⁻ 2013

At Issue

Child Pornography

Other Books in the At Issue Series:

At Issue

Child Pornography

Stefan Kiesbye, Book Editor

GREENHAVEN PRESS
A part of Gale, Cengage Learning

GALE
CENGAGE Learning·

Detroit • New York • San Francisco • New Haven, Conn • Waterville, Maine • London

Elizabeth Des Chenes, *Director, Publishing Solutions*

© 2013 Greenhaven Press, a part of Gale, Cengage Learning

Gale and Greenhaven Press are registered trademarks used herein under license.

For more information, contact:
Greenhaven Press
27500 Drake Rd.
Farmington Hills, MI 48331-3535
Or you can visit our Internet site at gale.cengage.com

Articles in Greenhaven Press anthologies are often edited for length to meet page require-ments. In addition, original titles of these works are changed to clearly present the main thesis and to explicitly indicate the author's opinion. Every effort is made to ensure that Greenhaven Press accurately reflects the original intent of the authors. Every effort has been made to trace the owners of copyrighted material.

Cover image © 1995–2007 Illustration Works, Inc. All rights reserved.

LIBRARY OF CONGRESS CATALOGING-IN-PUBLICATION DATA

Child pornography / Stefan Kiesbye, book editor.
    pages cm. -- (At issue)
  Includes bibliographical references and index.
  ISBN 978-0-7377-6157-3 (hardcover) -- ISBN 978-0-7377-6158-0 (pbk.)
  1. Child pornography. 2. Child pornography--Law and legislation. I. Kiesbye, Stefan.
  HQ471.C452 2013
  364.1'74083--dc23

                                                              2012046892

Printed in the United States of America
1 2 3 4 5 6 7 17 16 15 14 13

Contents

Introduction

In 2009, Matthew White, a twenty-two-year-old Californian from Sacramento, was charged with possession of child pornography, a crime that carried a possible twenty-year sentence. According to reporter Terrence O'Brien's December 7, 2009, article for the online magazine *Switched*, White claimed that he had downloaded the material from a file-sharing site by accident. He tried to download a *Girls Gone Wild* video, and when he discovered that the file really contained child pornography, he deleted it immediately from his hard-drive. A year later, FBI agents "showed up at the door and asked if they could examine the family's computer. The Whites agreed, and, at least at first, the agents found nothing incriminating. Not satisfied with their preliminary search, the agents used software to dig deep into the hard drive and to recover deleted files. There, they recovered the illegal images." According to White, the FBI acknowledged that he could not have accessed the deleted files himself, but regardless, he was charged with possession of child pornography. As O'Brien reports, "on the advice of his public defender, White is pleading guilty in hopes of cutting his potential 20-year sentence down to three and a half years. After serving his time, White will have to serve 10 years of probation and register as a sex offender."

To many, White's side of the story might sound as though he were someone who did actually possess and view child pornography but was in denial, trying to excuse inappropriate and illegal behavior. Stop It Now, an organization fighting to prevent child abuse, states on its website that "some people find themselves losing control over their use of pornography, for example by spending more and more time viewing it and, for some, looking for new and different types of pornography, including images of children. Some people accidentally find sexual images of children and are curious or aroused by them.

They may justify their behavior by saying they weren't looking for the pictures, they just 'stumbled across' them." At a time when awareness about child pornography is increasing, and parental fears concerning the Internet, social networking sites, and "sexting" are high, anyone who comes across a child pornography site might come under suspicion.

That's exactly what Nigel Robinson from Hull in the United Kingdom thought. He claims he was downloading music, when he discovered that he'd accidentally downloaded child pornography. Eric Limer, of Geekosystem.com, writes on March 7, 2012, that Robinson thought he had only two options. "Tell people [the police] about it or not. If he did the latter and got busted, he'd be in big, indefensible trouble. The former, however, doesn't seem to have been a better decision." Robinson did report his accidental download to the police, and even though an arrest wasn't made immediately, Robinson was barred from unsupervised visits with his daughter.

The climate of heightened suspicion and rapidly advancing law enforcement technology have raised questions regarding the point at which activity on the Internet becomes criminal. When a user visits—accidentally or not—a website with child pornographic content? Or when files, such as pornographic pictures or videos are downloaded? Stories like that of Nigel Robinson raise concerns about what to do if incriminating files—put there by accident or by malware—are discovered on computers. Deleting such files didn't help Matthew White, and alerting the authorities got Robinson into unforeseen trouble.

In May 2012, the New York Court of Appeals decided that a college professor was, according to Dan Nosowitz's May 5, 2012, article on Popsci.com, "found to have not committed an 'affirmative act' such as downloading, saving, or printing the [child pornography] image files in order to 'possess' them; rather, they were passively saved by his browser in its hidden cache." In other words, Internet users could not be held responsible for visiting pornographic sites, only for owning pornographic pictures.

Despite the ruling, the debate is far from over. While lawmakers and advocacy groups are scrambling to regulate computer use and prevent child pornography, they are aware that new, complex technologies will most likely provoke a complex debate over the issue. *At Issue: Child Pornography* discusses many aspects of this crime at a time when changing technologies are reshaping our culture.

1

Child Pornography Presents a Real and Growing Threat to Children

US Department of Justice

The US Department of Justice enforces the law and defends the interests of the United States according to the law. The Department aims to ensure public safety and provide federal leadership in preventing and controlling crime. An important part of the Department's mission is to seek just punishment for those guilty of unlawful behavior and to ensure fair and impartial administration of justice for all Americans.

Child pornography has seen a steep rise in recent years. The depiction of child sexual abuse has found its way onto countless websites, chatrooms, and file-sharing systems. Furthermore, since control of images once they are released electronically is virtually impossible, victims of child pornography will continue to suffer from distribution of humiliating pictures and videos. Because dissemination of illegal material has continued to become faster, easier, and cheaper, child pornography is a great danger our society must work hard to eliminate.

C*hild pornography* refers to the possession, trade, advertising, and production of images that depict the sexual abuse of children. The term *child pornography* is used throughout this Assessment because it is the legal and accepted term for

US Department of Justice, "The National Strategy for Child Exploitation Prevention and Interdiction." US Department of Justice, August 2010. www.justice.gov/psc/docs/natstrategyreport.pdf (March 10, 2012).

images of child sexual abuse; however, many experts in the field believe that use of that term contributes to a fundamental misunderstanding of the crime—one that focuses on the possession or trading of a picture and leaves the impression that what is depicted in the photograph is pornography. Child pornography is unrelated to adult pornography; it clearly involves the criminal depiction and memorializing of the sexual assault of children and the criminal sharing, collecting, and marketing of the images.

State and federal investigators and prosecutors universally report seeing dramatic increases in the number of child pornography images traded on the Internet, the number of child pornography offenders, and the number of children victimized by child pornography. They also report an increase in the sadistic and violent conduct depicted in child pornography images and that they are encountering more young victims than before—particularly infants and toddlers. In addition, law enforcement officers and prosecutors interviewed for this Assessment universally report connections between child pornography offenses and sexual contact offenses against children.

Child Pornography Is Easily Distributed

The Internet and advances in digital technology have provided fertile ground for offenders to obtain child pornography, share child pornography, produce child pornography, advertise child pornography, and sell child pornography. The Internet also has allowed offenders to form online communities with global membership not only to facilitate the trading and collection of these images, but also to facilitate contact (with each other and children) and to create support networks among offenders. Rather than simply downloading or uploading images of child pornography to and from the Internet, offenders also use current technologies to talk about their sexual interest in children, to trade comments about the abuse depicted in particular images—even as images are shared real-time—to validate each other's behavior, to share experiences, and share images of themselves abusing children as they do so....

Child Pornography Offenses Present a Real Threat to Children

The children whose abuse is captured in child pornography images suffer not just from the sexual abuse graphically memorialized in the images, but also from a separate victimization, knowing that the images of that abuse are accessible, usually on the Internet, and are traded by other offenders who receive sexual gratification from the children's distress. According to academic researchers, medical professionals, and child pornography victims themselves, knowing that all copies of child pornography images can never be retrieved compounds the victimization. The shame suffered by the children is intensified by the fact that the sexual abuse was captured in images easily available for others to see and revictimizes the children by using those images for sexual gratification. Unlike children who suffer from abuse without the production of images of that abuse, these children struggle to find closure and may be more prone to feelings of helplessness and lack of control, given that the images cannot be retrieved and are available for others to see in perpetuity. They experience anxiety as a result of the perpetual fear of humiliation that they will be recognized from the images....

Offenders can easily produce child sex abuse images using digital technologies and distribute the images over the Internet.

Child Pornography Is Increasing

Experts interviewed for this Assessment, most of whom have longtime experience in this area of law enforcement, concluded that the market—in term of numbers of offenders, images, and victims—has been trending significantly upward. . . .

Although documenting the precise quantity of child pornography is difficult, it is evident that technological advances have contributed significantly to the overall increase in the child pornography threat. Offenders can easily produce child sex abuse images using digital technologies and distribute the images over the Internet. From 2005 through 2009, U.S. Attorneys prosecuted 8,352 child pornography cases, and in most instances, the offenders used digital technologies and the Internet to produce, view, store, advertise, or distribute child pornography.

Prior to the mid-1990s, Internet access and the availability of digital home recording devices (still, video, and web cameras) were very limited, thereby confining the production and distribution of child pornography material to relatively few individuals. Today, the ease with which a person can move from viewing child pornography to producing and distributing child pornography is illustrated in numerous cases. In addition, advances in computer memory storage, the speed of downloading and uploading, and advances in file sharing technologies make it very easy to quickly transfer or receive large volumes of child sex abuse images. Numerous technologies are used by offenders—including P2P [peer-to-peer] networks, Internet Relay Chat (IRC), newsgroups, bulletin boards, photo sharing sites, and social networking sites, among others. Experts posit, and common sense suggests, that the easy accessibility to this material online draws new offenders to the crime.

As home digital recording and computer technology have improved and child pornography production and sharing have increased, so too have the illicit images and videos typically stored by offenders. Increased home computer storage capacity has enabled many child pornography offenders to store huge collections of images (some containing 1 million) and numerous video files (often 1 hour in length). For example, more than 15,000 stored videos were found on various media and the offender's computer in Philadelphia in 2007. Holding vast libraries of child pornography material enables offenders to share more illicit images and videos of greater variety than was possible in past years. . . .

The Thriving Market for Child Pornography Promotes the Fresh Abuse of Children

Most indicators reviewed by NDIC [National Drug Intelligence Center] for this Assessment point to a steady and significant increase in the volume of child pornography traded over the Internet, and they similarly suggest the existence of a large and global market. This growing and thriving market for child pornographic images is responsible for fresh child sexual abuse—because the high demand for child pornography drives some individuals to sexually abuse children and some to "commission" the abuse for profit or status.

> *Most indicators . . . point to a steady and significant increase in the volume of child pornography traded over the Internet, and they similarly suggest the existence of a large and global market.*

In one case, a predator victimized more than 150 children for profit before he was arrested by U.S. Postal Inspectors. In another case, the defendant was a "photographer" who traveled throughout several European countries to arrange, witness, and film the sexual abuse of approximately 20 underage girls. The "photographer" then sold the abusive images worldwide through his commercial web site. The initial exposure was estimated to have reached more than 3,000 active traders in approximately 28 countries. He also offered his customers the opportunity to make special requests for videos, purchase the child-sized lingerie used in some of the videos, and, in one case, the opportunity to travel to Europe to photograph the underage girls with him.

Another investigation revealed that offenders would congregate with like-minded people on the Internet and sometimes encourage each other to act out their fantasies and share proof. In Operation Hamlet, offenders abused their own children and made them available to other members of the group for the same purpose. Another case revealed that some child pornography offenders are driven to abuse children because providing new images to their online communities gives them "status." Some communities have restricted memberships, allowing entry only to those who contribute an image not already possessed by the group. In some instances, fathers have abused their own children, not out of any apparent sexual attraction to their children, but because they wanted to reap the benefits of producing and introducing a new child pornographic image into the market and their children were easily accessible targets.

In one highly publicized investigation, Federal Bureau of Investigation (FBI) agents interviewed a man who admitted molesting his daughter and videotaping the sometimes violent assaults. The child, who was 9-years-old when interviewed, said her father began assaulting her when she was 5-years-old. She said he would assault her and immediately publish the assaults on the Internet. The man told agents that he began molesting his daughter because he needed "fresh" images to provide others on the Internet before they would trade their own newest or least-circulated images with him. He described his desire for images he had not seen and said that, to get them, he was required to provide images others had not seen in trade.

2

As Child Porn Activity Grows, Efforts to Trap Offenders Do, Too

Tim McGlone

Tim McGlone has been a journalist for twenty years. He covers federal courts and federal law enforcement agencies, and has written about the death penalty and DNA issues. McGlone has won several journalism awards in New York and Virginia.

New technologies have made it easier for child pornographers to disseminate photos and videos of child sexual abuse, but law enforcement has adapted to the online distribution of illegal pictures, making strides in finding and prosecuting offenders. While there is no specific profile of a potential child pornography user, patterns of online use have emerged and give police insight into illegal activities. Still, while arrests have gone up, victims of violence and abuse are left to pick up the pieces and are powerless to stop the circulation of humiliating photos and videos.

Norfolk—Just six years out of high school, Daniel James Boynton ruined his life for a perverted thrill: He downloaded pictures of children being molested.

He knew what he was doing was wrong and illegal. He knew he was risking his rising Navy career. But he couldn't stop. Like many child pornography addicts, he organized his collection like a librarian arranges books, and his fetish grew more bizarre as time passed.

And like many offenders, Boynton had a sense of relief when he was finally caught. Already dishonorably discharged, he's now serving 12½ years in federal prison.

"I'd just like to say that I'm entirely sorry for what I did," he said at his sentencing. "I never had any intention of harming anybody."

The majority of [child pornography] offenders are white males, of all ages, with no criminal history or previous evidence of pedophilia.

His mother wept quietly in the back of Courtroom 2 in Norfolk's U.S. District Court that day in early December. His father, who did his best to testify for his son, appeared stunned.

"Total shock," Ben Boynton said, describing his reaction upon his son's arrest.

They thought they had raised him right. He had never been in trouble before. They were excited about his career goal of becoming a chef.

Boynton's case is iconic of most of the growing number of child pornography cases in state and federal courts. The majority of offenders are white males, of all ages, with no criminal history or previous evidence of pedophilia.

Researchers and therapists say the lure of child pornography, which grips addicts as intensely as crack cocaine, targets no singular class.

Offenders' educational and occupational backgrounds vary widely: They are convenience store workers and college professors, enlisted sailors and naval officers, police officers, the homeless, and even the FBI's own.

While the number of offenses seems small compared with, say, drug and fraud cases, child pornography was the fastest-growing crime over the past six years in Virginia—up 218 percent from 2003 to 2009.

Nationally, the picture is more startling: a 2,500 percent increase in arrests in 10 years, according to the FBI. U.S. Immigration and Customs Enforcement, which handles most federal child exploitation cases, has made 12,000 such arrests since the agency was formed in 2003.

U.S. Attorney Neil MacBride, whose office is handling more such cases each year, said child pornography was a dying industry until the Internet and peer-to-peer networks developed.

"It went from almost dead to now a growing epidemic," he said.

While the Internet has fueled the problem, increased law enforcement efforts have led to more arrests.

As a result of these joint efforts [between federal, state, and local authorities], more than 50 defendants were convicted in federal court here and sentenced to prison between March 2008 and August 2010, with prison terms ranging from one year to 40 years.

The problem is being attacked on several fronts by local, state and federal authorities and the military. Stopping it is one hurdle, but treating offenders could be even more difficult than catching them.

In a Peninsula office building, whose location the FBI wants kept secret, two agents troll the Internet looking for the worst of the worst child pornography offenders.

Agent Paula Barrows used to buy drugs as an undercover agent with the Illinois State Police in some of the most dangerous areas outside Chicago. She finds investigating child pornography more disturbing, but in a way more rewarding— maybe because she's a mom, too.

She's been doing this for nearly four years. The FBI mandates that she and anyone else assigned to child porn cases go through stringent psychological testing to make sure they can handle it.

"It's very graphic," she said of the pictures and videos she finds.

"They literally sicken you," her partner, Jack Moughan, said.

Together with agents from other federal agencies and local and state police, they operate a task force under a national program called Project Safe Childhood. There are similar ongoing federal efforts with names like Project Flicker and Operation Predator.

As a result of these joint efforts, more than 50 defendants were convicted in federal court here and sentenced to prison between March 2008 and August 2010, with prison terms ranging from one year to 40 years.

Some of the things they have discovered include: a father who dressed his toddler son up as a girl and filmed him in a sexual position; a sailor who searched for pictures of young boys being tied up and urinated on; and a Marine caught with 650,000 child porn images, some that can only be described as horrendous acts of bondage and bestiality.

Convenience store manager Jeffrey Lee Brackett, 56, is serving a 10-year prison term for transporting child pornography, which means he downloaded and shared images across state lines via the internet.

The Brackett investigation started like most others. In the summer of 2009, Barrows sat at her computer and launched the Lime Wire peer-to-peer program. Lime Wire had been the most prevalent P2P program used to share porn over the Internet until it shut down this fall under pressure from the government.

Barrows downloaded 33 files that appeared to be pornography (easily identified by their XXX names). Of those, 21 looked like child porn. One was labeled "real private daughter" followed by words including "lolita" and "preteen nude."

Had Barrows chosen any other file, she may have been led to another suspect. She'll often refer cases to her counterparts in other states.

"Our goal is clearly to target this area," she said.

In looking at the file, she could see that it was placed in a shared folder by someone identified only by an Internet protocol number. She then sent a subpoena to Cox Communications asking for the subscriber name on that number. Cox reported back that it belonged to Brackett's Newport News home. She obtained a search warrant and, with other task force agents, arrested Brackett.

After the arrest, she learned that Brackett had been fired after the convenience store chain's upper management discovered that he had been using a store office as his personal kiddie porn library and theater.

Law enforcement officials realize they can't arrest everyone viewing, downloading and trading child pornography.

Brackett seemed to be relieved. He had been in counseling for his addiction and knew he had a problem.

Over the past several years, Brackett had installed and uninstalled the P2P software because of his feelings of guilt. At first, he told agents that if there were images of child pornography on his computer, they got there by accident.

In the end, he admitted the truth.

Across the water in Norfolk, Immigration and Customs Enforcement agents do the same work. And just about every police department in the area now has detectives dedicated to stopping child exploitation.

All of this has led to a surge in child pornography arrests in the past five years. But law enforcement officials realize they can't arrest everyone viewing, downloading and trading child pornography. They estimate that 50,000 computers in the state contain child porn images.

ICE agents can only get to a couple of dozen a year in Hampton Roads.

"When we look at the end users, we look at those who pose a threat or those who act on it, by kidnapping a child, for example," said John Torres, special agent in charge of U.S. Immigration and Customs Enforcement for this region and Northern Virginia.

"Then it's those in a position of public trust, like teachers and police officers."

Because ICE and the FBI have overlapping jurisdictions in this area, ICE tries to focus on the international offenders— those who produce and distribute child porn from far away places like Russia—while the FBI zeroes in on domestic online predators.

Everything is getting cheaper and faster. It just proliferates the problem.

Producers and sellers of child pornography have been arrested in California, Pennsylvania, Florida, Spain, the Netherlands and Russia.

Local law enforcement agencies have formed their own task forces. The Bedford County Sheriff's Department in the western part of Virginia heads the federally funded Internet Crimes Against Children program that assists local task forces throughout the lower half of the state. The Virginia Beach Police Department coordinates those efforts for Hampton Roads.

Typically, detectives troll the Internet posing as children or acting as child porn collectors, said Sgt. Terry Wright of the Bedford County Sheriff's Department.

"I would say that the past few years it has grown exponentially," he said. "Everything is getting cheaper and faster. It just proliferates the problem."

A pattern he sees repeated in offenders is that they start with adult porn but get bored and turn to child porn.

Meanwhile, the Naval Criminal Investigative Service, Army Criminal Investigation Command and the other service law enforcement agencies have ramped up their efforts to root out child porn offenders in their midst.

Former Navy Petty Officer 1st Class Daniel J. Sweeney was sentenced to 41 months in federal prison and ordered to undergo intensive mental health treatment after he was caught buying $780 worth of child pornography while stationed aboard the Norfolk-based destroyer Mason and at other times.

Sweeney, arrested in Norfolk in 2008, was one of hundreds of service members and defense contractors targeted during an investigation dubbed "Operation Flicker."

Despite warnings from fellow crew members who witnessed his actions, Sweeney told federal agents "he was unable to control the compulsion to view and masturbate to images of child pornography," according to a statement of facts filed in court.

Flicker, started in 2006 by ICE, sought to dismantle Internet sites offering child pornography by subscription. Of the 5,000 customers ICE identified, 264 were affiliated with the Department of Defense, either as service members, civilian workers or contractors. Of those, 22 had top secret security clearance and an additional 54 had some form of secret security clearance.

That worries officials at the Pentagon because of the fear that enemies of the United States could try to blackmail those individuals.

After receiving criticism for going after only 52 of the 264, the Defense Criminal Investigative Service announced this fall that it was reopening its investigation into all the suspects but said that some would be dealt with administratively and not in the criminal courts because of a lack of resources or evidence.

Among those charged as a result of Flicker were a Navy lieutenant commander, an Army major, a number of lower-ranking sailors and soldiers, and Washington-area employees of the FBI and the National Security Agency. A related investigation also led to the arrest and conviction in Northern Virginia of the former director of the Department of Homeland Security's forensic laboratory.

The ultimate goals for all these agencies are to find as many child victims as possible, remove them from their abusive situations and stop the producers.

It's clearly an uphill battle.

The National Center for Missing and Exploited Children, which helps identify and locate children in pornography photos and videos, says its staff reviewed more than 10.5 million images in 2009 alone.

There are millions of users around the globe. Agents typically start with the user and try to work their way back to the producer and the victim. In one computer server alone, discovered in New Jersey, ICE agents found 60,000 users, Torres said.

It's lucrative as well: Distributors typically charge $80 for one file, though it appears most child porn is distributed over free file sharing networks.

And the number of victims continues to grow. The National Center for Missing and Exploited Children, which helps identify and locate children in pornography photos and videos, says its staff reviewed more than 10.5 million images in 2009 alone.

In 2002, the first year the agency began tracking down victimized children, two dozen kids were found. Since then, the agency has identified around 3,100 children who have appeared in photos and movies.

"There's still hundreds if not thousands of children out there" not yet identified, said John Shehan, executive director of the agency's exploited children division.

Reports of exploited children grow every year, he said. In 2009, the agency received more than 120,000 reports on its cybertip line. In 2010, the number grew to 160,000, with the vast majority being tips on child pornography.

Retired Marine William L. Judy of Virginia Beach is serving a 12-year federal prison term for possessing a staggering 650,000-image collection of child pornography meticulously organized and labeled. His attorney requested a 6½-year sentence.

What drives someone to collect child pornography, much less the vast amount Judy did, remains a mystery, according to researchers. The younger the children are, the more puzzling the behavior seems. Investigators say they are seeing more and more toddlers, and even infants, being molested.

What mental health experts have learned is that when someone becomes addicted to child pornography, he—and around 90 percent of offenders are male—often progresses to younger and younger children and will seek out sadistic or masochistic images and, in extreme cases, bestiality.

"It's hard to wrap your head around how that could be enticing to anyone," said Christopher Hummel, a private practice psychologist who also treats young sex offenders at The Pines, a youth psychiatric treatment center in Portsmouth.

"We know less about online child pornographers than many other types of offenders," wrote Michael L. Bourke, chief psychologist for the U.S. Marshals Service, and Andres E. Hernandez, a Bureau of Prisons psychologist.

"There are no evidence-based protocols to guide the assessment and treatment of these offenders," they said in their

2008 report studying child pornography convicts at the Butner, N.C., federal prison, one of three that treat such prisoners.

The study of 155 child porn offenders produced startling and controversial results. Before the report, it was believed that most offenders had never actually sexually abused a child.

Indeed, at the time of sentencing, 74 percent of those 155 inmates had no documented hands-on victimization of children. But by the end of treatment, 85 percent confessed to sexually molesting a minor at least once.

Hernandez, in a later paper, cautioned that their study is not conclusive and cannot be used to generalize all child porn offenders. Other studies have reported much lower rates of molestation.

Still, prosecutors have been urging judges to impose stiff prison terms as a way to deter potential abusers and repeat offenders.

Perhaps lost in many of these cases are the victims. These young children rarely show up in court to tell of the effects these rapes and photo images have had on their lives.

Chesapeake resident Neal Sabra, a repeat offender who was found with a thumb drive of kiddie porn attached to his key chain, received a 22-year prison term last summer. Williamsburg resident David Merritt, who has a prior child molesting conviction, was sentenced to 20 years in prison for trading child porn over the Internet.

Perhaps lost in many of these cases are the victims. These young children rarely show up in court to tell of the effects these rapes and photo images have had on their lives.

One girl, who was known as Misty in one of the more popular Internet child porn series, has sent her personal message to as many judges as she could.

"It is hard to describe what it feels like to know that at any moment, anywhere, someone is looking at pictures of me as a little girl being abused by my uncle and is getting some kind of sick enjoyment from it," she wrote to one Norfolk federal judge.

"It's like I am being abused over and over and over again."

3

Police Around the Globe Must Work Together to Fight Child Pornography

Paulo Fagundes

Paulo Fagundes is the director of the Federal Police of Brazil.

The police of Brazil have made great strides in combating producers and distributors of child pornography, but in order to fight online crime, which—by its very nature—is international, police and investigative services around the globe need to share information and work together. Sophisticated new technology used to detect and shut down child pornography can only be successful if it is allowed to reach beyond national borders.

Millions of children are developing virtual friendships around the world by connecting through the Internet. It is in this innocent environment that pedophiles are also aggressively targeting the relationship sites, instant messages, chat rooms, and file exchanges as tools to solicit children and teenagers. Law enforcement agencies all over the world have been detecting a massive and growing volume of file exchanges of content containing images of children or teenagers in pornographic or sex poses as pedophiles use the Internet to establish their illegal connections. Primarily these file exchanges today are occurring in the Peer-to-Peer (P2P) networks.

Peer-to-Peer Networks

Today, P2P networks are among the most popular applications on the Internet to facilitate file exchange among users, and the number of users participating in these networks keeps growing. In Brazil alone, it's estimated that 9.4 million people download music, movies, and TV shows utilizing P2P networks. Investigations have shown that these P2P networks, originally created for legal purposes, are heavily utilized to exchange illicit files such as child pornography and copyrighted material.

The attraction of P2P networks to the criminal is an unintentional consequence of the technical aspect between P2P technology and the conventional file exchange. P2P technology enables users to exchange files directly among themselves, without any support from, or connection to, a central server. This lack of a central hub has complicated investigations and facilitated illicit activities. When a central hub is used, the investigation focuses on the exchanges through the hub. With P2P, at any given time millions of computers could be connected to P2P networks, and this decentralization poses a great challenge to investigators.

Pornographers have driven the development of Internet technologies, including systems to verify online financial transactions and digital watermarking technology to prevent the unauthorized use of online images.

The Brazilian police received complaints about the illicit use of P2P networks, and an examination of these networks confirmed the severity of the child pornography problem using this technology. Not only are the P2P files exchanged among the pedophiles, these files are readily available to anyone. It is very easy to use simple keyword searches to find and download illicit content. Many files are named or tagged with apparently innocent keywords like "child" and "teen" which draws innocent users to the content. Parents have found that children and teenagers unintentionally download illicit content obtained through keyword searches. Juvenile users of P2P are at significant risk of inadvertent exposure to pornography.

Similar Patterns of Child Pornography Distribution

The scenario in Brazil is very similar to those reported in a study published by the U.S. Government Accountability Office called *Peer-to-Peer Networks Provide Ready Access to Child Pornography*. This study, published more than six years ago, reported that child pornography is easily found and downloaded from P2P networks. In one search using 12 keywords known to be associated with child pornography, 42 percent of the files were associated with child pornography images and 34 percent of the files were classified as adult pornography.

According to experts, pornographers have traditionally exploited and sometimes pioneered emerging communication technologies from the dial-in bulletin board systems of the 1970s to the World Wide Web in order to access, trade, and distribute pornography, including child pornography. Pornographers have driven the development of Internet technologies, including systems to verify online financial transactions and digital watermarking technology to prevent the unauthorized use of online images.

Brazil's Law Enforcement Solution

Stemming from several allegations received by the police, Brazilian officers started an investigation that confirmed the increase in the utilization of P2P networks for the exchange of child pornography. Aiming to curb this problem, the Brazilian Federal Police, utilizing the available expertise of its computer forensic examiners, developed the "EspiaMule" (SpyMule) tool, a software application capable of monitoring the pedophilia file exchanges in P2P networks. The software works primarily as a spy agent, sweeping the World Wide Web in search of people sharing pornographic content files involving children or teenagers, although any other type of files could be searched as well.

This tool, developed in-house by the Brazilian Federal Police computer forensic experts, is based on the networks utilized by the "eMule" application, which is highly popular in Brazil. The team realized the need for an automated and more efficient way of tracking online pedophiles and started developing a tracking tool that could aid future investigations. Because eMule is an open source application, the Brazilian Federal Police modified the source code to allow the filtering and identification of computers sharing files with illicit content. With a list of files proven to contain child pornography, the developed tool can be used to discover all computers presently connected to the eMule network sharing such files, anywhere around the world.

When it comes to online crimes, especially child pornography over the Internet, international cooperation is required because the Internet boundaries are vague, at best.

Cooperation Strategy

Two large operations, which became known as Carrossel I and II, were deployed based on the information gathered by the EspiaMule application. These operations were very successful and became references for employing a new paradigm in internal and international cooperation.

Internally, the collaboration among the Brazilian Federal Police members, represented by their criminologists (in this case computer forensic experts) and the investigative team made the difference. This collaborative work enabled the deployment of a very complex operation that was highly technical and very successful.

Internationally, several countries deployed similar operations as a result of records sent to Interpol by the Brazilian Federal Police, reaping excellent results in other countries as well.

When it comes to online crimes, especially child pornography over the Internet, international cooperation is required because the Internet boundaries are vague, at best. Outlawing the traffic of such files in a given country is useless, since the files will remain readily available through the Internet on computers located in other nations.

Results of Police Operations

The results of these two large operations deployed in Brazil are reflected in many other countries. The information collected by the EspiaMule application was sent to Interpol, and over 400 search warrants were served worldwide. More than 100 arrests were reported, and at least four children were saved from sexual abuse by adults—in addition to the confiscation of hundreds of thousands of illicit content files. . . .

In total, almost 200,000 unique users were found in a 12-day search period worldwide. In the case of the Carrossel I and II operations, specific filters were used so only the most relevant users (active and with the highest number of shared files) for this investigation were selected. . . .

Cooperation Is the Key

In a great example of initiative and ingenuity, the Brazilian Federal Police developed an innovative application to aid in its investigations and evidence collection, allowing the gathering of information to subsidize large operations in the fight against Internet child pornography file sharing.

The development of this application and its utilization in large operations have proved to be key ingredients to the success obtained through partnership and collaborative work be-tween criminalistics, represented by the federal criminology experts of the Brazilian Federal Police and investigations, en-abling police operations in areas that required advanced tech-nical knowledge.

Besides the example of internal collaboration and synergy, the international collaboration, through Interpol, was crucial in this fight against Internet child pornography and many other crimes.

There is still much to do, for instance, expand the software to support other file-sharing networks and become useful in other countries where different networks have become more popular.

4

Bath Time Photos Prompt Child Porn Allegations

Dan Przygoda, Sarah Netter, and Desiree Adib

Dan Przygoda, Sarah Netter, and Desiree Adib are journalists, producers, and frequent contributors to ABC News, *covering a broad range of social topics.*

The desire to protect children from exploitation and sexual abuse can lead to parents being prosecuted for harmless nude pictures of their children. In a culture wary of sexual predators and the danger of online child pornography, suspicion and misinterpretation have already caused harm to parents and their children, and laws designed to protect young children might end up actually hurting them.

For A.J. and Lisa Demaree, the photos they snapped of their young daughters were innocent and sweet.

But after a photo developer at Walmart thought otherwise, the Demarees found themselves in a yearlong battle to prove they were not child pornographers.

"I don't understand it at all," A.J. Demaree told "Good Morning America" Monday. "Ninety-nine percent of the families in America have these exact same photos."

The eight photos in question were among a batch of 144 family photos the Demarees had taken to their local Walmart. The developer alerted the police and the investigation into child pornography began in earnest, even though the parents maintained they were innocent bath time photos.

The Peoria, Ariz., couple had their home searched by police and worse, their children—then ages 18 months, 4 and 5—were taken from them for more than month. Their names were placed on a sex offender registry for a time, and Lisa Demaree was suspended from her school job for a year. The couple said they have spent $75,000 on legal bills.

Perversion is in the eye of the viewer.

A report issued by local authorities described the photos as "child erotica" and "sex exploitation," the couple's lawyer Dick Treon told "Good Morning America." He said the person responsible for the report was unqualified to make such judgments.

The Demarees are now sharing a few of the photos with the public, he said, so the "truth can catch up with the lie."

"These photos were never intended for anyone to see except for family members," Treon said. "Perversion is in the eye of the viewer."

Eventually, a judge threw out charges against the Demarees, but now they're going on the legal offensive by suing the state, the city and Walmart for their role in what they call a "nightmare."

"I think that we need to have an awareness of how our innocent photographs can be misconstrued and misperceived," Lisa Demaree said.

The Demarees are suing the city of Peoria and the State Attorney General's office for defamation. They're also suing Wal-Mart for failing to tell them that they had an "unsuitable print policy" and could turn over photos to law enforcement without their knowledge.

"At Walmart, we're committed to providing quality service and convenience to our photo customers," the company said in a statement. "These are sensitive allegations and we're taking them very seriously."

"It was unbelievable. I was in so much disbelief. I started to hyperventilate. I tried to breathe it out," Lisa Demaree told "GMA" this weekend, struggling through tears. "Some of the photos are bath time photos, but there are a few after the bath. Three of the girls are naked, laying on a towel with their arms around each other, and we thought it was so cute."

Lisa Demaree told "Good Morning America" today that the girls seem to be doing well, but that her oldest is showing some signs of anxiety when she visits other people's homes. She calls her experience in state care as time at the "stranger's house."

We have told our girls that they have freedom to be in their home and feel OK about their bodies and their nudity, but that there is a time and a place for it.

"They're doing really well, I think, considering what happened," she said. "But sometimes we don't know the effects that children experience and are undergoing when they go through things like this."

After Walmart alerted them, investigators went to the Demaree home to question them and search their residence where the children live with their parents.

A.J. Demaree said he could understand why the police were there, but he said the pictures were innocuous snapshots of his kids goofing around, and some of them involved the children being naked.

"We have told our girls that they have freedom to be in their home and feel OK about their bodies and their nudity, but that there is a time and a place for it," Lisa said.

Police seized numerous videotapes and the Demarees' computers and said they found more photos and videos of the children frolicking without clothes.

Investigators and Child Protective Services saw it very differently and removed the children from the house.

A medical exam of the children revealed no signs of sexual abuse, and a judge ruled that the photos were in fact harmless.

ABC News legal expert Dana Cole said that in cases of child pornography authorities need to prove sexual intent on the part of the parents, and that after the judge reviewed the case and the Demarees underwent psychological evaluation, it was determined that there was no such intent.

From the Demarees' perspective, the damage was already done.

Police and prosecutors insist they did what they thought was appropriate.

"It took us a long time to take a picture [again]," Lisa Demaree said. "I even worry about them in their bathing suits now, if I get a shot of them in their bathing suits and they're tilting their heads a certain way or their hips are sticking out a little bit, all I think of is 'Does someone think that it was posed? Or how is that going to be perceived?'"

Steve Meissner, a spokesman for Child Protective Services, released a statement saying, "When a police agency calls us on a matter, we have an obligation to act on that matter. If we refused, the community would be very unhappy with us."

The city of Peoria also states that it stands behind the appropriate actions of their officers.

"Honestly we've missed a year of our children's lives as far as our memories go," Lisa Demaree said, "As crazy as it may seem, what you may think are the most beautiful innocent pictures of your children may be seen as something completely different and completely perverted."

ABC News' Lee Ferran contributed to this report.

5

Child Protection Laws Might Lead to Privacy Violations

Conor Friedersdorf

A staff writer at The Atlantic, *Conor Friedersdorf is also the founding editor of* The Best of Journalism, *a newsletter devoted to exceptional nonfiction writing.*

In an attempt to fight child pornography, lawmakers have come up with a bill that—if passed—would give law enforcement agencies unprecedented access to private online accounts and would violate users' rights. While child pornography is a serious issue, the public should be wary of new laws that might infringe on their Internet privacy. If new legislation is passed too quickly and without proper safeguards against abuse, it might end up doing more harm than good.

Every right-thinking person abhors child pornography. To combat it, legislators have brought through committee a poorly conceived, over-broad Congressional bill, The Protecting Children from Internet Pornographers Act of 2011. It is arguably the biggest threat to civil liberties now under consideration in the United States. The potential victims: everyone who uses the Internet.

The good news? It hasn't gone before the full House yet.

The bad news: it already made it through committee. And history shows that in times of moral panic, overly broad legislation has a way of becoming law. In fact, a particular moment comes to mind.

Broad New Laws Can Do Serious Harm

In the early 20th Century, a different moral panic gripped the United States: a rural nation was rapidly moving to anonymous cities, sexual mores were changing, and Americans became convinced that an epidemic of white female slavery was sweeping the land. Thus a 1910 law that made it illegal to transport any person across state lines for prostitution "or for any other immoral purpose." Suddenly premarital sex and adultery had been criminalized, as scam artists would quickly figure out. "Women would lure male conventioneers across a state line, say from New York to Atlantic City, New Jersey," David Langum explains, "and then threaten to expose them to the prosecutors for violation" unless paid off. Inveighing against the law, the *New York Times* noted that, though it was officially called the White Slave Traffic Act (aka The Mann Act), a more apt name would've been "the Encouragement of Blackmail Act."

That name is what brought the anecdote back to me. A better name for the child pornography bill would be The Encouragement of Blackmail by Law Enforcement Act. At issue is how to catch child pornographers. It's too hard now, say the bill's backers, and I can sympathize. It's their solution that appalls me: under language approved 19 to 10 by a House committee, the firm that sells *you* Internet access would be required to track all of *your Internet activity* and save it for 18 months, along with *your* name, the address where *you* live, *your* bank account numbers, *your* credit card numbers, and IP addresses *you've* been assigned.

Police State Tactics Are Looming

Tracking the private daily behavior of everyone in order to help catch a small number of child criminals is itself the noxious practice of police states. Said an attorney for the Electronic Frontier Foundation: "The data retention mandate in this bill would treat every Internet user like a criminal and threaten the online privacy and free speech rights of every American." Even more troubling is what the government would need to do in order to access this trove of private information: ask for it.

I kid you not—that's it.

In Communist countries, where the ruling class routinely dug up embarrassing information on citizens as a bulwark against dissent, the secret police never dreamed of an information trove as perfect for targeting innocent people as a full Internet history.

As written, The Protecting Children from Internet Pornographers Act of 2011 doesn't require that someone be under investigation on child pornography charges in order for police to access their Internet history—being suspected of any crime is enough. (It may even be made available in civil matters like divorce trials or child custody battles.) Nor do police need probable cause to search this information. As Rep. James Sensenbrenner (R. Wisc.) says, "It poses numerous risks that well outweigh any benefits, and I'm not convinced it will contribute in a significant way to protecting children."

Among those risks: blackmail.

Government Should Not Have Unfettered Access to Private Information

In Communist countries, where the ruling class routinely dug up embarrassing information on citizens as a bulwark against dissent, the secret police never dreamed of an information trove as perfect for targeting innocent people as a full Internet history. Phrases I've Googled in the course of researching this item include "moral panic about child pornography" and "blackmailing enemies with Internet history." For most people, it's easy enough to recall terms you've searched that could be taken out of context, and of course there are lots of Americans who do things online that are perfectly legal, but would be embarrassing if made public even with context: medical problems and adult pornography are only the beginning. How clueless do you have to be to mandate the creation of a huge database that includes that sort of information, especially in the age of Anonymous and Wikileaks? How naive do you have to be to give government unfettered access to it? Have the bill's 25 cosponsors never heard of J. Edgar Hoover [longtime FBI director known for using questionable methods to obtain information on those he considered radical or subversive]?

You'd think that Rep. Steve Chabot (R-Ohio), who claims on his Web site to be "an outspoken defender of individual privacy rights," wouldn't lend his name to this bill. But he co-sponsored it! You'd think that the Justice Department of Eric Holder, who is supposed to be friendly to civil libertarians, would oppose this bill. Just the opposite. And you'd think that lots of tea partiers, with all their talk about overzealous government and intrusions on private industry, would object.

But they haven't.

As [American writer and journalist] Julian Sanchez recently wrote on a related subject, "In an era in which an unprecedented quantity of information about our daily activities is stored electronically and is retrievable with a mouse click, internal checks on the government's power to comb those digital databases are more important than ever. . . . If we aren't willing to say enough is enough, our privacy will slip away one tweak at a time."

6

Child Pornography Laws Must Not Compromise Free Speech

Duane Gundrum

Duane Gundrum is the author of thirteen novels. He is a writer, professor, and former counterintelligence agent and computer game designer.

The case of an unsavory book's legal battle makes it clear that free speech is imperiled by overeager law enforcement officials. While published texts might be offensive to many, police and prosecutors should not be allowed to use the public's outrage to restrict freedom of expression. Child pornography is a serious threat, but the expression of even offensive ideas—as opposed to illegal actions—should be protected. Civil rights are too precious to be dealt with lightly.

An interesting thing happened a few months back that was barely even observed other than the usual outcries from the general population. Some guy wrote a really stupid book that basically explained how to be a pedophile, and he wrote it from some weird perspective of someone trying to protect children. Now, I won't go into the positives and negatives of this, as I'm sure people can come to their own opinion rather quickly, but what happened was there was an outcry the second this book ended up on Amazon's book lists. People made such an outcry that the book was immediately pulled from Amazon, and all attempts to get further information about it were met with zero results. What's interesting, that is not really being shared very often in the later stories, is that there were 3,011 customer reviews of the book. Now, I don't know if there were 3,011 customers before it got pulled, or if those are just the usual yahoos making comments after the facts got out, or even if they were positive or negative, but it sure does make one think.

Sadly enough, the marketplace of ideas has always been a murky one when it comes to the area of children.

Freedom of Speech

Anyway, that wasn't the end of the story. Turns out that a Florida sheriff decided he needed to put together a "sting" operation that consisted of going online and buying the book by mail. Once the book was delivered, he issued the arrest warrant, and Mr. Phillip Greaves was picked up in Colorado by police there. Now, we're about to find out exactly how free a country we live in.

You see, there's more going on than some child porn creator being arrested. Well, actually, it's not even child porn, come to think of it. What it is, although I am going off of other reports as I've never read the book myself, is a book filled with ideas of the guy who wants to show how to date kids and do it in a positive way, whatever that might actually mean. Either way, he's going to get his day in court, and we're about to find out how illegal his activities actually were.

Because there were no kids actually involved, so this is going to be a trial about ideas. But sadly enough, the marketplace of ideas has always been a murky one when it comes to the area of children. Pretty much everything else has been defended by the Supreme Court, including most types of por-

42

nography, ranging from Roman orgies to blood splattering S&M [sadism and masochism]. But what has never really been defended is anything involving children.

The Supreme Court Avoids the Issue of Child Pornography

But the reason it hasn't been defended is not mainly because the Supreme Court has felt such activities deserve no protection, but that government has done a pretty good job of avoiding actually getting cases to the Supreme Court, because in case you don't know it, the laws that involve suppression of anything involving children are way off the charts when it comes to freedom of speech and civil liberties. Always, the defense is "it's for the children" but rarely is it so important for the children that they're willing to take cases all the way to the highest court, unless they're so sure of a supreme dunk that they won't risk anything else.

The reason for that is, if they lost one of these cases, a whole lot of criminal systems would come tumbling down, as would a lot of potential careers of prosecutors who make a living off of fighting child smut. Always, they can rely on the average American to back them up with "that's just horrible stuff" that they don't have to do much to fight any defense against their one-sided actions.

Violating Civil Rights

This case might actually be very interesting in that some serious violations of civil rights have been done here all in the name of the children. And really, the only defense of those violations is "it's for the children" and "anyone who would do that is just scum". And funny enough, I agree with them. But the Constitution was never meant to be judged on those merits. It's judged to be like the blind naked woman that an attorney general decided to cover up for modesty. It's supposed to be blind and not concerned about the moralistic side of the house. Justice has to be blind, or it's never really justice.

Which brings up some other issues that are going to start coming to light soon, which is kind of funny because they're also being fought in the realm where Wikileaks exists. If the morality police win this time, what happens is that anyone can now be liable for pretty much anything he or she writes anywhere that someone gets something published. Because all that has to happen is some jurisdiction somewhere in the United States has to not like something, and sure enough all they have to do is get their hands on it, and the person who wrote it is now liable for charges if some jurisdiction has made it illegal.

Justice has to be blind, or it's never really justice.

Going Down a Slippery Slope

So, if some sheriff in Louisiana decides he doesn't like any kind of writing that criticizes a political party, all he has to do is get his common thinking local government to agree with him, then go access this information on the Internet, and it's now been "delivered" to him, so he can now order the government police in the jurisdiction of Michigan or California to arrest that person so he can be charged back in Louisiana. Um, I said Louisiana as an example, so sheriffs of Louisiania, please know that I love you (in a good and LEGAL way) and you don't have to arrest me for anything I've said.

There is a huge slippery slope that has been created here that no one even realizes, or even cares about, because they always foolishly think, oh it won't be used THAT way. Well, we thought that same thing when we enacted the Patriot Act, and does anyone remember what the first action taken under that act was? Anyone? Well, it turns out the Patriot Act was used to arrest a bunch of Democrat legislators who were running away from Texas to avoid voting on a redistricting plan. The Patriot Act allowed the federal government to "arrest" them and bring them back to Texas to force them to vote. Kind of leaves a warm, fuzzy feeling inside, doesn't it? Because that's what's called a slippery slope because people once they get a bit of power tend to use it to do things they weren't originally given the power to use it for in the first place.

That's the slippery slope.

So, you can think this guy is scum, and he probably is, but as [with] the cases of most of our Supreme Court cases involving pornography, some of the rights that newspapers like the *New York Times* hold dear came from some pretty unsavory people doing some pretty unsavory things, and it took the Supreme Court [to accomplish that], acting against the common sense of the people because they realized the beneficiaries would be those same people many years later. Unfortunately, I don't think our Supreme Court may act the same way again as it is now filled with a lot more partisan judges who are looking at their political views before their constitutional ones. Let's hope they are as forward thinking as some of their forefathers.

Until then, let's all go after this guy like a pack of rabid dogs. After all, we're the unwashed rabble that makes up the population. That's what we do best.

7

Online Child Pornography Can Harm Victims for Life

Adriana M. Chávez

Adriana M. Chávez is a police and court reporter for the El Paso Times.

For victims of child pornography, the ordeal of having been abused and exposed to hundreds or thousands of Internet users may never come to an end. Even once the sexual abuse suffered at the hands of family or strangers has ended, pictures and videos are still available to users of child pornography and their distribution cannot be controlled. In the age of the Internet, the emotional burden of being humiliated and violated in front of a camera may never be erased.

Each time someone views videos of "Vicky" as a child being raped by her father, old wounds are opened anew.

"Vicky," as she is referred to in federal court documents, can't stand the thought that, even 10 years later, someone might recognize her on the street, at school or at work.

Instead, living with the knowledge that strangers are viewing the series of videos her father taped over three years, beginning when she was 10 years old, she has decided to make those who download those videos pay.

Asking for Restribution

She wants them to pay for her therapy, the job wages she's lost, the attorney's fees she's had to pay and for the trauma she's endured.

Across the country, in U.S. courthouses, she's filed dozens of requests for restitution against those who have either pleaded guilty or have been federally convicted of downloading the videos. At least two of those cases involve people in the El Paso area. One has already been ordered by a federal district judge to pay Vicky and other victims $150,000 in restitution.

In all, Vicky is seeking restitution in more than 80 federal cases and is asking for a total close to $1 million.

On Friday [September 30, 2011], U.S. District Judge Frank Montalvo sentenced Luis Enriquez-Alonso, 26, to five years in prison for downloading child pornography while at home and at the University of Texas at El Paso, where he was attending school.

Upon his release from prison, Enriquez-Alonso, who is originally from Mexico, must be on supervised release for the rest of his life. Court filings show Enriquez-Alonso has already made arrangements to pay the $150,000 in restitution.

Abused by Her Father

Immigration and Customs Enforcement agents, along with investigators from the Texas Department of Public Safety, arrested Enriquez-Alonso after finding more than 5,400 images and 128 videos depicting child porn on his two laptop computers and other computer-related media. Some of those videos featured Vicky, who had been filmed by her father performing various sex acts with him. In a few instances, Vicky's father made her act out scripts he wrote.

Vicky's father was sentenced to 50 years in prison. His real name, along with Vicky's real name, have been redacted from court documents filed in the Enriquez-Alonso case and the case of another 26-year-old El Paso resident, Chad Redenius.

Court records show Redenius pleaded guilty in April to possession of child pornography. In August, Senior U.S. District Judge David Briones sentenced Redenius to 10 years in prison, followed by 10 years of supervised release.

The fact that each one is out there and has seen me and watched me being raped makes me sicker, makes me feel less safe, makes me feel more ashamed and more humiliated.

During Redenius' last court hearing, federal prosecutors and his attorney indicated they are working on an agreement to pay Vicky restitution. Redenius is appealing his sentence.

Vicky's Seattle-based attorney, Carol Hepburn, couldn't be reached for comment, but last year she told the *Billings Gazette* in Billings, Mont., that movies and photographs of Vicky are considered to be among the most widely circulated images of child pornography. Vicky, who is now in her early 20s, has been identified by the National Center for Missing and Exploited Children in about 8,000 cases.

In a victim-impact statement written by Vicky and filed in the cases of both Redenius and Enriquez-Alonso, Vicky states each time a defendant either pleads guilty or is convicted of downloading her videos, she receives a notice.

"The Notice puts a name on the fear that I already had and also adds to it," Vicky wrote in her statement. "When I learn about one defendant having downloaded the pictures of me, it adds to my paranoia, it makes me feel again like I was being abused by another man who had been leering at pictures of my naked body being tortured, it gives me chills to think about. The fact that each one is out there and has seen me and watched me being raped makes me sicker, makes me feel less safe, makes me feel more ashamed and more humiliated."

The Danger of Being Exposed

Vicky also stated she fears the men who have viewed her videos may want to contact her. In a few instances, some have via Facebook or MySpace after learning her true name.

In the prosecution's request for restitution, federal prosecutors state Vicky suffers from panic attacks and insomnia, and has difficulty holding a job or going to school because of frequent panic attacks.

"While she continues to try to live a normal life, 'Vicky' carries emotional burdens which continually get in her way," prosecutors stated.

8

New Technology Makes It Easier to Distribute Child Pornography

Linda Trischitta

Linda Trischitta has been covering crime and the people it impacts for the Sun Sentinel *since 2007. She writes the "Crime & Safety Blog" and is a member of the* Sun Sentinel's *breaking news team. Her work has also appeared in the* Times Union *in Albany, New York,* People Magazine, *and* Reader's Digest.

Through the quick rise of the Internet, cell phones, and tablet computers, child pornography producers have been able to trade illegal material faster and reach a wider audience. Furthermore, predators have found new ways to hide their true identities and approach children and adolescents by creating fake online profiles. Law enforcement agencies around the nation have tried to keep pace with new developments, and while there has been an increase in child pornography, arrests have gone up as well. However, only if police can successfully answer the challenge posed by mobile electronics will the increase in child pornography be stopped.

Internet technology and mobile devices are expanding the ways predators can approach children and child pornography is traded and sold, investigators say.

Increased online sharing of illegal images has prompted a sharp rise in tips to law enforcement agencies, and police say they are making more arrests. In 2010, the 595 tips about online child porn and other forms of child exploitation in South Florida showed an 85 percent increase from 2009, according to a federally funded task force.

At the same time, the victims are getting younger.

"Most [offenders] are collecting images of kids under 5 years old, infants and babies, with sound," said Dennis Nicewander, a prosecutor who runs Broward County's Sex Crimes Child Abuse Unit.

Prosecutors once relied on physicians to testify that a victim was underage. But Nicewander says he doesn't have to call on medical experts because it's so obvious the kids are not young adults.

Nicewander says the users' appetites have gotten harder to allay.

"They're no longer satisfied with a 5-year-old, they want a 2-year-old, something more graphic. And they videotape it while they're doing it. This entire culture has developed that treats children as sex objects. And all of that goes into the increase in cases."

Creating Fake Online Profiles

Though tips and prosecutions are up, so are the ways determined offenders can get to children. By pretending to be kids themselves, they use fake screen names, steal child photos and create biographies with local schools and activities that seem familiar to the targeted child.

The good news: Approaches through a family's favorite online electronics—laptop, tablet, cellphone or video gaming system—can be turned into evidence against the predators.

Think your child is safe from Internet solicitations because the family computer is in the living room or kitchen?

"That's an obsolete concept, because the child most likely has a smartphone in his pocket," said Kenneth Lanning, a retired special agent with the FBI from Fredericksburg, Va.

Forces arrayed against online child pornography include the National Center for Missing & Exploited Children, federal and state prosecutors and 61 federally funded task forces dedicated to investigating Internet crimes against children (ICACs).

Think your child is safe from Internet solicitations because the family computer is in the living room or kitchen?

Florida has three, based in Polk County, Gainesville and Fort Lauderdale. South Florida's task force is composed of federal, state and local officers from more than 50 agencies that serve from Key West to Fort Pierce and west to Collier and Lee counties.

The task force's 155 child exploitation arrests in 2010 are a nearly 10 percent increase from 141 arrests during the previous year.

"Child pornography is on the rise and that's what we've been making arrests for, in the past two years," said Broward Sheriff's Sgt. Giuseppe Weller, a supervisor of the South Florida ICAC task force. He said "travelers" who would arrange to meet a minor for sex have become wise to "Dateline" Catch a Predator-type stings that the Broward Sheriff's Office also conducted, from 2007 to 2009.

"They research their victims more thoroughly to make sure it's not a cop pretending to be a teen," Weller said.

Victims' Pictures Are Widely Distributed

Offenders may think they are avoiding that risk by viewing illegal online content, but there is still a victim in every image that can be traded hundreds of times.

"Advanced investigative techniques showed us how bad child porn was getting, so we shifted our focus," Nicewander said.

In 13 years of prosecutions, Nicewander says his team lost just one of its 300 cases. They are working 50 more through the court system.

Most offenders will plead guilty, he says, and only six of those 300 closed cases have gone to trial because of the amount of prosecution evidence that police gather.

Catching a Predator

How is a user of online child pornography caught?

The federal government requires electronic service providers like AOL, Gmail, photo-sharing sites like Flickr and Shutterfly, and social networks like Facebook and MySpace to report incidents of child sexual exploitation that include child pornography or solicitations of minors for sex.

Those reports are sent to the National Center for Missing & Exploited Children, which vets and forwards the cyber tips to the task forces, Immigration and Customs Enforcement, U.S. postal inspectors, the FBI and police in other countries.

Beyond the fact that most are male, there is no such thing as a profile of a person who collects or makes child pornography, investigators say.

That reporting system may have led to the indictment in September [2011] of South Florida's Immigration and Customs Enforcement regional leader Anthony Mangione on charges of possession, receipt and transportation of child pornography. His home computer was seized last spring after AOL reportedly called in a tip.

The federal, state and local investigators who talked for this story said they are not involved in the case against Mangione, who has pleaded not guilty.

Beyond the fact that most are male, there is no such thing as a profile of a person who collects or makes child pornography, investigators say.

He can be the guy next door or someone prominent. Convictions have been obtained against teachers, religious leaders, police officers, executives and media figures, including a sports announcer for the University of Florida.

"It's a human being who has a sexual interest in children," said Lanning, who still advises the FBI and consults nationally on crimes against children. "The person doesn't necessarily have to have a prior arrest, have molested children, or been a predator financially profiting from the crime."

Desktop or mobile devices with fast Internet connections and a lot of storage space make it easier for users of child pornography to maintain their collections—and find like-minded friends.

"With the Internet, I don't care what disgusting, perverted thing you're interested in, you'll find 1,000 people [online] who will validate it," Lanning said.

Experts say an offender generally can't use the defense of just being curious about child porn.

For an applicant to gain entry into the online chat rooms that peddle these images, site managers may demand videos or photos of children being abused.

And sharing files that may contain hundreds of images can lead to trafficking charges and prison sentences that can last decades.

But prosecutors can win cases on much less evidence.

"One photo of a child being tortured or molested is a felony," said Weller of the ICAC task force. "And one is enough."

9

New Technology Can Help Arrest Child Pornography Users

CBS Miami

CBS Miami is a local affiliate of CBS Broadcasting Inc. (CBS), the second largest television and radio broadcaster in the world.

To stem the rising tide of electronically shared child pornography, the police have found new ways to do fast forensic examinations of electronic evidence and arrest pornography users. New technologies have helped distribute illegal pictures and videos, but they are also used to combat Internet-savvy child pornography producers.

The state's latest tool to clamp down on child pornographers might not look like much from the outside—a plain-looking white van.

But investigators say the van has enhanced their operations by allowing them to put handcuffs on suspects much more quickly.

One morning in mid-January [2012]—after a pre-dawn planning session—investigators from the Internet Crimes Against Children, or ICAC, task force drove the van into a quiet, working class Margate [Florida] neighborhood.

Catching Child Pornographers

Their target was a man suspected of downloading and sharing explicit images of "very young children under the age of 12 engaging in various sex acts" with adults and children, according to an arrest report.

The suspect, George Baram, emerged from his house wearing a shirt that read, "It's your lucky day." For Baram, it turned out to be anything but lucky.

As agents from the ICAC carried computers, hard drives and compact discs out of Baram's home, technicians began sifting through the computer hardware in the van.

We can now conduct a search warrant and make a decision and take the predator off the street so they can no longer prey on children and exploit them.

Within a short time, they discovered the videos.

An arrest report shows that Baram confessed, saying he downloaded the videos then deleted them. Baram told investigators, "that he has never touched a child in a sexual manner."

Mike Phillips, FDLE's Chief of the Computer Crimes Center, said the van enables agents to do time-consuming forensic examinations on the spot, which is a major change.

"Before we were having to leave suspects out on the streets until we could fully look at all the evidence," Phillips explained. "We can now conduct a search warrant and make a decision and take the predator off the street so they can no longer prey on children and exploit them."

Phillips said there is a "significant increase" in child pornography cases statewide and because of the heavy caseload, Phillips said that in the past it could take up to a year to examine a suspect's computer.

An Increase in Arrests

Stats from FDLE [Florida Department of Law Enforcement] show that in 2011, the agency made 1,076 arrests in child pornography cases statewide. In 2008, that number was 749.

The van is assisting agents to deal with the caseload, Phillips said. He added that it also encourages confessions. While agents in one section of the van are examining the computer equipment, they can confront the suspect, who is seated in another section, with the images of child pornography found on his computer.

"We have had suspects break down and cry," Phillips said. "We've had suspects that become defiant, that want us to learn why this is ok. Because in their minds they truly believe that abusing children sexually is normal."

FDLE also has more agents at its disposal in their fight against child pornography.

Last summer, agents from the state attorney general's office joined forces with FDLE. The agents were spread across the state and it resulted in an increase of 6 officers fighting crimes against children in South Florida.

"It allows us to share intelligence, share training, share information much more quickly than when we were having to be in separate offices," Phillips said.

The ICAC is comprised of agents from 57 agents across South Florida and into Naples. The task force is federally funded and is headed by the Broward Sheriff's Office.

New Technology Helps Law Enforcement

The van has been a welcome addition to the efforts to curtail the downloading and sharing of child pornography. With all the latest technology inside, the vans cost about $100,000 and there are three of them operating statewide.

The van sat quietly outside George Baram's home in Margate as cyber detectives built their case against him.

We spoke to George Baram briefly after he was handcuffed and led to a waiting unmarked police car. When asked why he was being arrested, Baram initially denied downloading child pornography. Then he said, "You download stuff, music, sometimes file names are mislabeled."

When asked if he watched the videos of child pornography that investigators say they found on his [computers] he told CBS 4 News, "I delete them."

FDLE, meanwhile, said they expect more arrests as they use this van to continue the task force's crackdown on child pornography.

"For some of these people they may be on the verge of actually molesting a child," said Bob Breeden, FDLE Assistant Special Agent in Charge. "For every person that we can take off the street that's involved in child pornography, [there] may be one child that doesn't get victimized."

FDLE agents say parents need to pay close and constant attention to the online activities of their children. FDLE recommends a website—secureflorida.org—which has safety tips and important information for keeping track of the websites your child visits and their passwords.

10

Child Pornography Could Be Planted on a PC but It Is a Minimal Threat

Larry Magid

Larry Magid is a journalist and Internet safety advocate who has been writing and speaking about Internet safety since 1994, when he wrote the Internet safety guide Child Safety on the Information Highway. *He is founder of SafeKids.com and SafeTeens.com, and a co-director of ConnectSafely.org. Magid has also served as a board member of the National Center for Missing & Exploited Children.*

At a time when viruses and botnets—a network of computers taken over by malware—have infiltrated many home computers, the fear of a virus planting child pornography in one's files is legitimate; but while such a scenario is a real possibility—as shown by a recent case of a state employee being falsely accused of child pornography use—it is not very likely to happen. Malicious software has the capability to plant disturbing images on a person's hard drive, providing a standard excuse for people arrested under the suspicion of buying or trading child pornography, but forensic investigators have ways of determining responsibility. Nevertheless, people should use anti-malware software and take other precautions to safeguard themselves from potentially devastating cyber attacks.

A story recently surfaced saying malware could plant child porn on innocent people's computers without their knowledge. Just how real is this threat? And how can you keep it from happening to you?

Being accused of possessing child pornography can ruin people's reputations, confront them with overwhelming legal bills and, if convicted, deprive them of their freedom for years if sentenced to prison time, and perhaps for life, if they're required to register as sex offenders.

That is why, at least in part, a recent case outlined by the Associated Press [AP] raised concerns over computer viruses being used to plant child pornography on people's computers. But the innocent have little to fear, according to experts.

The Computer Virus Threat

The AP story reported about the case of Michael Fiola, a former Massachusetts state employee whose state-owned work computer was found to contain illegal child pornography images. He was fired and charged with possession of child pornography which, had he been convicted, could have landed him in prison for up to five years, according to the AP.

Sexually explicit images of children—who are often being exploited—are not protected by the First Amendment because they may memorialize, celebrate, or encourage sexual crimes against children deemed defenseless victims. Although Fiola avoided a child porn conviction, he reportedly has suffered related indignities, including death threats and friend abandonment. The AP said he and his wife liquidated their savings and spent $250,000 on legal fees.

Ultimately, charges were dropped after Fiola's defense showed that his computer was infected by a virus that was "programmed to visit as many as 40 child porn sites per minute," something that a human couldn't do, even if he or she tried. Other reports about this case indicate that the antivirus software on Fiola's computer was out of date and therefore was not protecting him against malware.

The Danger of Malicious Software

How likely is a case like Fiola's? If viruses are capable of putting illegal content on people's computers, aren't we all at risk of being arrested for serious crimes we never meant to commit? And if it is possible for this to happen, isn't "the virus did it" claim likely to become the mantra of every defense attorney who represents people accused of possessing child pornography?

To help answer these questions, I spoke with security experts, legal scholars, former prosecutors, and Justice Department officials. The consensus? It is indeed possible for malicious software to plant child pornography—or any other type of file, for that matter—on an innocent person's computer, but being possible doesn't mean it's likely. And forensics experts can detect intention.

"It's quite possible for a malware creator to include child pornography as part of the payload on an infected computer," according to Symantec spokeswoman Marian Merritt, but "such payloads are not typical."

If viruses are capable of putting illegal content on people's computers, aren't we all at risk of being arrested for serious crimes we never meant to commit?

Most malware authors, Merritt said, "are motivated by money, and there's no clear indication as to how planting child porn on an unsuspecting person's computer would help generate money for criminals."

One possible motive for remotely using someone else's computer to store child porn is to make it possible to access the contraband without running the risk of it showing up if your PC is seized or searched. Merritt worries that "this could become a possible use for malware, going forward," but

Michael Geraghty, executive director of the National Center for Missing & Exploited Children Technology Services Division, said that, while possible, it's not an effective way to store child porn and remain undetected.

The Use of "Zombie Machines"

"If you put the images on someone else's computer, you might not be able to retrieve them when you want them," Geraghty said. He pointed out that the zombie machine storing the data would have to be turned on and connected for the malware sender to access it. If it weren't online, or the files had been deleted, the files wouldn't be there to retrieve.

Another deterrent, of course, is a potential digital trail between your computer and the one you're using to store it. Although there are ways to evade detection, forensic investigators do have ways to trace Internet Protocol addresses to catch people in the act of uploading and downloading material.

"I've never seen it where child porn was intentionally placed on someone's computer because of a virus," Geraghty said. He has, however, seen cases where "someone was redirected to a site where it could have entered the cache." If someone were to go to a legal adult porn site, it's possible that the browser would "open 100 different windows," including some that could contain child porn. "As a result of that, any images on any of these sites would be cached, and there would be a record that you had been there."

But Geraghty said investigators can tell the difference between someone who deliberately downloaded such images and someone who may have inadvertently downloaded perhaps thousands of images because of a virus or misdirected Web site.

Totality of Evidence

"A good forensics expert would try to determine how (the images) got on the computer and who was responsible for putting them there," he said. "That would be determined by looking at the totality of the evidence, not just the fact that there were images there."

Things a good investigator would look into include whether the suspect was sitting at the computer at the time the images were downloaded. Was he using the computer to send e-mail or visit other Web sites at the time? "There is always some type of trail we can follow to determine if the person were likely actively involved in the process of downloading the material," Geraghty said.

Another indicator is the time lapse between image downloads. A virus or Trojan horse is likely to download multiple images at a time, sometimes faster than might be humanly possible to do manually. A person who collects child pornography typically acquires it over a period of time, and a forensic investigation of the computer should reveal that.

Phil Malone, a clinical professor at Harvard Law School and director of its Berkman Center Cyberlaw Clinic, agrees that a good forensic investigator should be able to tell the difference between files placed by a virus and ones deliberately downloaded.

There is always some type of trail we can follow to determine if the person were likely actively involved in the process of downloading the material.

"It's the excuse of the moment for defendants," he said. "Lots of child porn defendants try to blame (images found on their computers) on viruses, but it's almost never true. You can actually figure this out. In the handful of cases that have been problematic, it looks as if everyone moved too quickly. The agency discovered material and immediately jumped to conclusions." Malone added that "good, solid forensics would be able to tell in virtually every case."

Malone agreed with Geraghty, of the National Center for Missing & Exploited Children, that it's fairly common for someone, when viewing adult pornography on a Web site, to inadvertently receive pop-ups that may include images of child porn.

"It's possible to tell if something was opened or saved to a file from the cache," Malone said. Investigators can usually figure out if an image was downloaded intentionally, based on other activity that took place on the computer at the time, he said, adding that it's incumbent on both prosecutors and defense attorneys to launch a thorough investigation that includes analyzing a copy of the hard drive to determine not just which images are stored within, but also how they got there.

Geraghty said it's important to look at other factors. "The computer holds a lot of information about the searches that someone runs. If there were none of those searches and nothing else but some images in the cache, you would question how they got there. You would look for collaborating evidence such as intent to visit the site (and capability) of visiting the site. Did he have knowledge?"

A good investigation will look for exculpatory evidence to see if there are other explanations for the images. That investigation, Geraghty said, should start with making one or more exact copies of the suspect's hard drive and examining those copies to look for evidence of malicious software that could be responsible for the images. Defense attorneys can also gain access to a copy of the drive, but because it may contain illegal child porn images, their experts will probably have to examine the drive at the police station or prosecutor's office; possession of those images—regardless of the reason—is illegal for anyone other than personnel granted immunity.

Burden of Proof

"In each case, the prosecution will need to prove (that) the defendant knowingly and intentionally possessed, received, or distributed child pornography," according to Drew Oosterbaan, chief of the Child Exploitation and Obscenity section of the Justice Department. "The proof starts with establishing that the images involved are child pornography and ends with establishing that the person charged is criminally responsible for it. We prove the latter in myriad ways."

Oosterbaan said that when someone is charged with possessing child pornography on his computer, "the computer is, in many ways, a crime scene, and the forensic examination of that computer is critical to meeting the elements of proof in the prosecution." He added that "it's important to remember that in every case, the government carries the burden of proof."

Oosterbaan said he is not aware of any cases in which botnets were used to plant child porn on other people's computers.

A former federal prosecutor now working for a technology company, who requested anonymity, said this may become a bigger issue as we enter the era of cloud computing, in which more and more data is stored on Internet servers instead of hard drives.

The computer is, in many ways, a crime scene, and the forensic examination of that computer is critical to meeting the elements of proof in the prosecution.

"There is no question that perpetrators are going to look for places to hide their criminal activity, including child porn, because they're increasingly aware that if law enforcement comes to their house, they will see the material," the former prosecutor said, adding that companies in the cloud storage business need to be aware that their systems could be used for illegal purposes. "They should reach out to the National Center for Missing & Exploited Children to implement a system to compare uploaded files against hash marks (digital fingerprints) of known child porn images."

As with any other security issue, the best defense is to protect your machine against intrusions.

- Making sure that your operating system and regularly used software are up-to-date.

- Using good software addressing malware, phishing attacks, and/or spam, and keeping it up to date. Subscriptions to paid programs should be renewed.

- Being cautious about spam and about providing information to sites you navigate to from links within even the most legitimate-appearing e-mails.

11

Adult Pornography Leads to Consumption of Child Pornography

Patrick A. Trueman

Patrick A. Trueman was chief of the US Department of Justice, Child Exploitation and Obscenity Section, Criminal Division in Washington, DC, from 1987 to 1993. He is president of the non-profit organization Morality in Media.

In order to effectively combat child pornography, government officials need to turn their attention to the largely ignored problem of adult pornography. While law enforcement has chiefly focused on arresting and prosecuting child pornography producers and users, adult pornography goes unpunished and is abundantly available to Internet users, including teenagers. Once bored of hardcore adult pornography, users seek out ever more bizarre material and turn to child pornography. If the government wants to address the growing problem of child pornography, it also needs to shut down illegal adult outlets and prosecute its producers.

Since President [Barack] Obama took office, the Department of Justice has not initiated one adult pornography criminal case. The reason, we are told, is that investigators are overwhelmed with child pornography cases. Problematically, a growing number of law enforcement officers and investigators report that consumption of adult pornography leads to consumption of child pornography.

The link between adult and child porn is observed globally, and it is nothing new. Fifteen years ago, at the 1996 World Congress against Commercial Sexual Exploitation of Children, Margaret Healy stated in a paper titled "Child Pornography: An International Perspective" that "with the emergence of the use of computers to traffic in child pornography, a new and growing segment of producers and consumers is being identified. *They are individuals who may not have a sexual preference for children, but who have seen the gamut of adult pornography and who are searching for more bizarre material.*" (Emphasis added)

Since the advent of the Internet age, millions of federal and state tax dollars have been channeled toward fighting Internet child pornography.

Ten years ago, Muireann O'Brian also observed this in her work with child sexual abusers. She heads the Bangkok office of End Child Prostitution in Asian Tourism, a global organization that helps police and lawyers target child molesters. She pointed out that "*arrests have shown men with perfectly normal sexual proclivities become seduced, then involved and finally addicted to child pornography.* Their addiction may manifest itself by them just keeping and looking at the images. . . . But it has been found that the addiction leads many men into seeking out children to abuse." (Emphasis added)

A Surge in Child Pornography Cases

Today, a simple Google search of news articles demonstrates that what Healy and O'Brian saw years ago is now common. In a 2008 story describing the increase of child sex crimes in Spain experts attributed the surge in such crimes to Internet opportunities. "The web not only provides an outlet for people with deep-rooted pedophiliac tendencies, but can also create a sexual attraction to children," Guillermo Canovas explained. He pointed out that "studies show that some pedophiles feel attracted to children from an early age, but the majority of them develop the tendency later on. . . . Thousands of people are constantly looking for pornography on the web . . . as their stimulation threshold rises, they feel the need for stronger and stronger material until their search leads them to child pornography."

The congressionally-created Child Online Protection Act (COPA) Commission saw the need to curb adult obscenity as a necessary precursor for combating child pornography. It included a recommendation in its 2000 *Final Report* "that Government at all levels fund aggressive programs to investigate and prosecute violations of obscenity laws. . . . This investigation and prosecution program should supplement the Government's existing effort to investigate and prosecute child sexual exploitation, sexual abuse, and child pornography. . . . Such a program should be of sufficient magnitude to deter effectively illegal activity on the Internet."

Since the advent of the Internet age, millions of federal and state tax dollars have been channeled toward fighting Internet child pornography. Like many government programs, those targeting child pornography are on autopilot, gobbling up ever-increasing resources with no critical evaluation of effectiveness. Rather, "success" seems to be counted by the number of arrests and convictions. By that measure, law enforcement successes climb every year, regardless of the safety of our nation's children. No credible claim is made that children are safer today than at the beginning of the Internet age. The number of child pornographers is increasing, not decreasing. According to the Bureau of Justice Statistics, the main sex exploitation offense referred to U.S. attorneys shifted from sex abuse (73%) in 1994 to child pornography (69%) in 2006.

Child pornography matters accounted for 82% of the growth in sex exploitation matters referred from 1994 to 2006.

Adult Pornography Must Be Prosecuted

The U.S. Department of Justice must change course and begin vigorously to enforce adult as well as child pornography laws. Additionally, no researcher has yet published a study that uses empirical science to validate the link between adult and child pornography that so many who fight child pornography and molestation have observed. The U.S. Department of Justice doles out hundreds of millions of dollars for crime research, ostensibly to discover ways to make us safer. The link between adult and child pornography should now be a top target of research. Presidential candidates should pledge that their attorney general will make this happen.

Children are harmed not only by child pornographers, but also by the consumption of adult pornography. The average age of a child's first exposure to pornography is 11. A total of 90 percent of children ages 8-16 have viewed pornography online. Many are becoming addicted to freely available Internet pornography. The effects of pornography are powerful on their developing brains. Eric M. Johnson, a clinical psychologist and full-time forensic evaluator who directs the Oregon Forensic Institute says that some children who encounter pornography "are captured by the images." Johnson treats kids in trouble for sexual behavior and has observed how his patients use the Internet to view pornography: "For them it becomes something very different, and they become obsessed. They think about it all the time . . . and so it begins to dominate their lives." There is also evidence that the rise in child-on-child sexual abuse appears to flow from consumption of Internet pornography.

Since the Internet came into its own nearly 20 years ago, Congress has tried to protect children from online pornography through the Communications Decency Act (CDA) and

COPA. Unfortunately, the United States Supreme Court has declared both laws unconstitutional. The acts would have removed "teaser" porn from the front pages of Internet pornography sites. This kind of material induces those whose eyes it catches to pay for more material beyond the front page. Under these acts, adults seeking porn could procure it only by providing credit card or other information that a child would not have. Children would not see any pornography on the sites.

When these acts were stricken, Congress seemed to give up on attempts to protect children from pornography on the Internet. Remarkably, it seems that no one at the top level in the Department of Justice has considered that the one effective—and constitutional—way to protect children from harm would be the vigorous prosecution of illegal, hardcore adult pornography. Federal laws prohibit distribution of hard-core adult pornography (called "obscenity" in law) on the Internet, on cable/satellite TV, through the mail or common carrier, in retail shops, and on hotel/motel TV. A handful of companies control large numbers of porn sites, so a few well-placed prosecutions would go a long way in gleaning up the Internet, where most kids find hardcore pornography.

> *Children are harmed not only by child pornographers, but also by the consumption of adult pornography.*

A Change of Strategy

Is the protection of children from pornography a government responsibility? Yes, of course it is. Practically speaking, no parent can watch over his or her children 24 hours a day. Even when parents utilize pornography-blocking software in their own home, kids will have access to the material at friends' homes or even at many public libraries. The predatory pornography industry targets children with their teaser material, including entire websites distributing volumes of hardcore porn for free.

Parents need help, and since the Congress has seen fit to outlaw distribution of obscene Internet pornography not only to children but to adults as well, why should parents not be able to rely on authorities to enforce the law? Who is it that gave the DOJ a pass simply to look the other way, dismissing the will of Congress and helping pornographers target our kids? It is time to reconsider this informal grant of immunity to the porn criminals and think first of the welfare of our children.

Candidates for president must pledge to protect our children from pornography and that means committing to the vigorous prosecution of illegal adult pornography as well as child pornography.

12

Pornography Is an Addiction

Aleah Taboclaon

Aleah Taboclaon is a mental health counselor and trainer, as well as a writer and editor of fiction and nonfiction work. Her articles have been published in national daily newspapers, on websites, and in magazines.

Watching child pornography is even more harmful than it may seem, because many offenders are also child molesters. Yet in order to combat the problem of child pornography, society needs to understand that pornography is an addiction and, as such, a brain disease. Modern brain monitoring devices have shown that pornography users' brains react in the same ways that drug users or gambling addicts do. Only widespread understanding of the danger, scope, and pervasiveness of pornography can lead to effective treatments.

For quite some time, men have defended their addiction to pornography by saying that they are just using it and not acting on it. But is pornography really as harmless as some would like us to believe?

Pornography Consumption and Sexual Abuse

In a study (2000) done by Andres Hernandez, director of the Sex Offender Treatment Program in the US Federal Correctional Institution in Butner, North Carolina, he found out that the majority of offenders convicted of Internet sexual crimes (specifically child pornography) have similar behavioral characteristics with those convicted of child molestation.

In fact, he said, 76 percent of offenders convicted of child pornography had "contact sexual crimes" and seemed to have committed sexual offenses more (i.e., 30.5 victims per offender) than those who were convicted outright of contact sexual crimes. Results of a more recent study by Hernandez (2009) have also shown that a lot of Internet child pornography offenders are also child molesters.

How Pornography Addiction Works

Psychologists have long debated about the appropriateness of associating pornography with addiction, pointing out that there are no diagnostic criteria in the DSM-IV [*Diagnostic and Statistical Manual*] regarding porn consumption.

Other mental health professionals and neurology researchers, however, strongly agree that those who are hooked on pornography behave like addicts and should be treated as one. Mary Anne Layden, PhD, for example, said that increasing tolerance to addictive substances is a key feature of addiction. Porn addicts develop this, needing more and more pornography materials (increasing either the intensity or the frequency of use, or both) to get the same high.

To understand this tolerance better, brain scanning technologies have been used through the years to provide an objective measure of how addiction affects the brain. Unlike self-reports, which are highly subjective and difficult to collect, tools like the functional magnetic resonance imaging (fMRI) can look directly into the brain and "read" how addictive substances—including pornography—affect it.

Dr. Nora Volkow, Director of the US National Institute on Drug Abuse (NIDA), is the pioneer when it comes to brain imaging studies. Her papers established how addictions physically alter the brain's physiology through changes in the neurochemical composition of the brain's frontal regions. These areas are responsible for regulating the motivation, drive, and pleasure impulses, and determine how addicted people think and feel when exposed to addictive substances.

Use of the fMRI in Addiction Studies

The fMRI had been discovered in the early 1990s but it only became increasingly used in addiction studies a decade later. It functions the same way as the MRI—a tool using a strong magnetic field and radio waves—but instead of taking pictures of the body's organs and tissues, it tracks the brain's blood flow.

Researchers using the fMRI to study psychological phenomena monitor changes in the brain's blood flow while the research participants are subjected to a specific stimulus—a pornographic image, for example, in the case of a porn addict. The results would then show which parts of the brain are activated when the stimulus is shown.

Years of research work at the [National Institute on Drug Abuse] using the fMRI has shown that instead of just being a compulsion, addiction is a brain disease.

Addiction Is a Brain Disease

Years of research work at the NIDA using the fMRI has shown that instead of just being a compulsion, addiction is a brain disease. Continued exposure to addictive substances—such as food, drugs, alcohol, or pornography materials—releases neurochemicals that rewire pathways in the brain and affect decision making. It results in increased cravings for the substance and creates a dependency that requires more stimulation.

Studies have shown, for example, that it is the brain's frontal lobes which are affected by these chemicals. When there is a pleasurable stimulus, the brain releases dopamine, which then activates the brain's reward center and produces pleasurable feelings. With a porn addict's continued exposure to these stimuli, there is a reduction in the amount of dopamine, resulting in the increased demand for the chemical.

The addicted person, whose dopamine receptors are already desensitized, must then find ways to increase the dopamine levels in the brain to feel good. In the case of porn addicts, more and more extreme pornography materials become needed through time to produce pleasure.

Changes in the brain due to pornography addiction can also be explained through studies on learning and memory. Julie Malenka and Robert Kauer (2007) called these "long term potentiation" and "long term depression," where brain cells are changed and rewired with the constant search and evaluation of pornographic materials.

Findings of another study (2007) done in Germany on pedophilia showed that brain changes in pedophiles are similar to those who are addicted to substance abuse and food, providing further evidence that sexual compulsions including porn addiction can cause changes in the brain.

Researchers say that if porn addiction is a disease, it follows that it can be treated.

Implications for Treatment

There are a lot more studies showing the connection between addiction and how it changes the brain. What does this all imply, in relation to treatment?

Researchers say that if porn addiction is a disease, it follows that it can be treated. But treatment doesn't start without recognition and admission on the part of the person that he or she has a problem with pornography.

However, the need for recognition that pornography harms should not only stop with the individual; the society needs to do it as well, for any global effort to curb the effects of pornography to be effective.

13

Child Pornography Users Should Be Given Therapy as Well as Punishment

Lou Michel

Lou Michel is the lead crime reporter at the Buffalo News. *During his more than two decades as a journalist he has won Associated Press awards, given interviews to local and national radio and television programs, and made appearances on* Good Morning America *and* ABC World News Tonight.

What is often overlooked in the discussion about child pornography is the pain and suffering of the families of those convicted of owning or trading illegal pictures. Many family members are unaware of the criminal activities their husbands or children are involved in, and when these crimes come to light families are subsequently ostracized by neighbors and their communities. However, new support groups try to assist those family members and advocate for laws that would help first-time offenders receive a second chance. However, in an atmosphere of suspicion and outrage, many citizens and politicians don't want to be seen as forgiving of child pornography and don't seek to rehabilitate pornography offenders. Only if society seeks to understand and help offenders will there be an effective way to treat pornography addiction.

They are seen as social lepers but still loved by their spouses and parents.

What these husbands and sons have done is considered criminal and reprehensible: collecting and viewing pornographic images of children.

The illegal behavior is almost unfathomable for their relatives to comprehend. Offenders often end up in federal prison, while their loved ones are left to rebuild shattered families.

It is a task, they say, that cannot be done alone.

CAUTIONclick ... supports laws that would give first-time offenders a second chance.

Taking Action

And that is why Western New York has become home to one of the country's first support groups for relatives of individuals convicted of possessing child pornography.

"We tell our children, 'Don't text and drive,' or, 'Don't talk on your cellphone and drive,' but I never thought to tell them, 'Stay away from porn on the computer.' We didn't know child porn was any more illegal than adult porn," said Marty, a father whose 25-year-old learning-disabled son is in federal prison.

Bill, whose 27-year-old son is serving eight years in a federal prison, says he sometimes views himself as a failure as a parent.

"It makes you feel like, where did you go wrong? We missed it, and we're still kicking ourselves," he said.

The two middle-aged fathers are members of CAUTION-click, and if you knew their full names they would be crushed. The shame and embarrassment of this happening in their families is that overwhelming.

Of course, their sons' names have been reported in the media, but the hope is that others in the community have since forgotten.

And so CAUTIONclick abides by the anonymity tradition of Alcoholics Anonymous, using only first names when publicly promoting the group.

Each month, 20 to 25 of the group's members from as far away as Rochester and the Southern Tier gather at a private meeting place in the Buffalo area and open up their hearts.

In addition to providing one another with emotional support, CAUTIONclick—which stands for Citizens Against Unfair Treatment of Internet Offenders Nationwide—supports laws that would give first-time offenders a second chance.

Instead of being sentenced to several or many years in federal prison, offenders would receive extensive counseling and be spared the label of sex offender on a state registry.

Some Child Pornography Offenders Can Be Helped by Counseling

Marie, who is married to Bill, says there is a big difference between "hands-on sex offenders" and "noncontact offenders." And yet they are all lumped together, with individuals who molest children sometimes spending less time in prison.

At a recent group meeting in her well-kept suburban home, Marie recalled nearly collapsing in her kitchen when her adult son told her he was under investigation for possessing child pornography.

"He came over a week later and told us federal agents took his computer from his apartment. Out of 100 Internet sites he visited, four were deemed to have underage pornography," she said.

Marie and other group members believe their loved ones, with proper counseling, will never again look at any type of pornography.

David G. Heffler, a Lockport psychotherapist who counsels sex offenders, says not all who view child pornography are cut from the same cloth.

Some find themselves viewing it as the result of becoming jaded to adult pornography and seeking new levels of excitement. He calls that the slippery slope.

Others, however, have an interest in children from the start and can be labeled "pedophiles" who present a much greater risk, Heffler said.

The individuals in the former group, Heffler said, could benefit from long-term, community-based treatment rather than lengthy prison sentences, though he believes there must be consequences for viewing child pornography.

Determining who is a "high-risk deviant" rather than someone who slipped into viewing child pornography, he said, would require consultation with mental health professionals under the supervision of the courts.

As for CAUTIONclick, Heffler says there is a place for that type of support group, but its members need to have a balanced view and recognize that some people who turn to child porn are genuine threats to children.

She still loves her husband, despite the hardship his behavior has inflicted on the family.

Finding Emotional Support

Advocacy aside, the group's members say they help each other to deal with the wreckage left behind by their loved ones. Jeannie, who also has a 27-year-old son in federal prison, says she still breaks down in tears, though it has been two years since the FBI raided her home.

Yet at her first meeting of CAUTIONclick, she says Marie's words were just what she needed to hear.

"She told me, 'You are not alone,' and that was lifesaving," Jeannie said.

Kate, a mother of three young children, tells group members how she has had to scramble working a full-time job as an office manager and keeping the family together since her 40-year-old husband was sentenced to five years in federal prison.

"I knew he had issues with pornography. It had been an ongoing issue for us," said Kate, adding that she was not totally shocked when federal agents showed up at their house early one morning three years ago.

She still loves her husband, despite the hardship his behavior has inflicted on the family.

For the year that his case was pending in federal court before he took a plea deal, she said, "It was the best year of our marriage. He was getting counseling."

Exposure to pornography is almost inevitable. We're surrounded by it. The brain's pleasure center is hijacked by it.

Kate and other members say their loved ones started out with adult pornography and eventually ended up viewing child pornography. If adult pornography had not been mainstreamed into society, they say they might not be in this painful situation.

"A sexualized society" is how the group's volunteer moderator, Carol Conklin, describes current-day culture.

"Exposure to pornography is almost inevitable. We're surrounded by it. The brain's pleasure center is hijacked by it. First it is vanilla porn, then people move on, not really discriminating. They're like in a trance," said Conklin, a licensed clinical social worker who has devoted her practice to sexual addiction counseling. "I've seen lives and families destroyed by the impact of all the issues related to hypersexuality."

To make her case that society has gotten out of control when it comes to boundaries that would spare children, Conklin holds up a recent issue of *People* magazine in front of the group members gathered at Marie and Bill's dining-room table.

On the cover is a glossy image of a 5-year-old beauty queen. The headline asks: "Gone Too Far?" and points out that children are wearing skimpy costumes in beauty pageants.

Those who would lust over a sexualized image of a child, says Jeannie, are sick.

Instead of sending them to prison, why not get them help? she asks.

Helping Offenders Overcome Addiction

"What do we do with sick people in this country—get them help or lock them up with zero chance of redemption?" she said.

Whether CAUTIONclick members will succeed in modifying the laws is difficult to say.

They have sent petitions to the U.S. Sentencing Commission, seeking a review of the recommended sentencing guidelines for child pornography possession and have attempted to meet with politicians.

Most politicians refuse to meet, not wanting to appear soft on the issue of child pornography, according to Marty, the father of the learning-disabled convict.

Marty's wife, Cheryl, says, "Everyone who reads this story about us will probably think, not me, but it could be."

14

Teen Sexting Should Not Be Prosecuted as Child Pornography

David Walsh

David Walsh is the author of Why Do They Act That Way? A Survival Guide to the Adolescent Brain for You and Your Teen. *He is also the founder and president of the National Institute on Media and the Family.*

The panic over sexting has clouded the judgment of state legislators and officials. In an ill-advised attempt to combat this risky practice, they have handed out draconian punishments and prosecuted as child pornographers teenagers who have sent nude pictures of themselves. Sexting is a new phenomenon and instead of criminalizing teenagers' behaviors, society should educate them about appropriate use of new technologies. Instead of harsh sentences, patience and education are needed.

Text messages are forcing us to rethink the way we deal with the difficult issues that arise when teenagers get involved with sex. . . . Some in law enforcement have taken extreme measures against teens who send sexually explicit words and images using cellphones and Internet sites. Their solution? Treat these kids just like adults who traffic in pornographic pictures of children.

For instance, 19-year-old Philip Alpert will remain on the Florida Department of Law Enforcement's Sexual Offender

Registry until he is 43 because he sent several dozen people a nude picture of his 16-year-old ex-girlfriend—a photo she sent to him first. In Pennsylvania, three girls, 14 to 15, sent three boys, 16 to 17, naked pictures of themselves. All six kids were charged with child pornography.

The Panic on Sexting

During the past year, more than two dozen teens in at least six states have been investigated by police for sexual texting, or sexting, the sending or possession of sexually charged photos or messages. A recent "Sex and Tech" survey by the National Campaign to Prevent Teen and Unplanned Pregnancy found that about one in five teens have sent nude or semi-nude pictures or videos of themselves. Sexting, it turns out, is all too common.

As the prevalence of sexting cases continues to come to light, many states are grappling to determine an appropriate punishment for this frightening new trend. With no federal law on the books, kids committing the same act in different states are finding themselves facing drastically different, sometimes life-altering, punishments.

Right now the laws in different jurisdictions are inconsistent, confusing and, in some cases, ridiculous.

In Ohio, sexting is considered a felony. If convicted, a person could face years in prison and is required to register as a sex offender. Just a few states away in Missouri, under proposed legislation, sexting would be classified as a misdemeanor. In Illinois, lawmakers recently passed an anti-sexting bill that would not charge the person who is in the photo, but rather anyone who forwards the message to a third party without consent.

Confronting New Technologies

For parents, this new trend is no doubt alarming. It is important to bear in mind that teen brains are still undergoing development. Impulse control, the ability to weigh consequences and hormonal-emotional spikes are not the same for adults and teens. Making matters even more complicated, much of our technology, including text messages, is fairly new. As a society, we are still working through our standards.

As parents, we need to take responsibility for monitoring our children's technology use. Regularly check your child's Facebook and MySpace profiles. Know what text messages your kids are sending and receiving and who they are communicating with online. Talk to your kids about sexting and make sure they realize what the consequences are even if they do not get caught. Sexual photos are rarely only seen by the original recipient. In the Sex and Tech survey, one-third of teen boys said they have had nude or semi-nude images, originally meant for someone else, shared with them.

Our laws need to catch up with this technology. Right now the laws in different jurisdictions are inconsistent, confusing and, in some cases, ridiculous. In some states, for example, a conscientious parent who finds a provocative picture of his daughter while checking her cellphone could be charged with a felony for viewing child pornography. I believe that there should be a consequence to get kids' attention, but teen stupidity merits a misdemeanor, not a life-ruining felony.

As a nation, we have to rise to the occasion if we want our children to fully understand what sex really means in a young person's life. Sexy videos on TV and racy sites on the Internet tell kids sex is no big deal. Some state officials are teaching them it's criminal in the extreme. If we want them to grow up to be happy, healthy adults we need to give them guidance and clear standards.

Organizations to Contact

The editors have compiled the following list of organizations concerned with the issues debated in this book. The descriptions are derived from materials provided by the organizations. All have publications or information available for interested readers. The list was compiled on the date of publication of the present volume; names, addresses, phone and fax numbers, and e-mail and Internet addresses may change. Be aware that many organizations take several weeks or longer to respond to inquiries, so allow as much time as possible.

AntiChildPorn.Org (ACPO)
website: www.antichildporn.org

AntiChildPorn.org is an organization comprising volunteers from all around the world. Its mission is to stop the sexual exploitation of children. ACPO addresses the issues of child pornography production and distribution via the Internet, as well as the predatory use of the Internet for the sexual abuse of children. News, links to like-minded organizations, and other resources are available at ACPO's website.

Association of Sites Advocating Child Protection (ASACP)
5042 Wilshire Blvd., Suite 540, Los Angeles, CA   90036-4305
website: www.asacp.org

Founded in 1996, ASACP is a nonprofit organization dedicated to online child protection. ASACP battles child pornography through its Reporting Hotline and helps parents prevent children from viewing age-restricted material online with the Restricted To Adults (RTA) website label. Tips, news, and statistics are offered on its website.

Institute for Responsible Online and Cell-Phone Communication (I.R.O.C.2)
PO Box 1131, 200 Walt Whitman Ave.
Mount Laurel, NJ   08054-9998

(877) 295-2005
website: www.iroc2.org

I.R.O.C.2 is a nonprofit organization advocating digital responsibility, safety, and awareness. It endorses the development and safe use of all digital devices and the Internet. The organization's mission is based on the fact that many individuals are not aware of the short and longterm consequences of their actions when utilizing digital technologies. Articles on social networking and sexting are available at its website.

National Association to Protect Children (NAPC)
PO Box 27451, Knoxville, TN   37927
website: www.protect.org

NAPC is a national pro-child, anti-crime membership association established in 2004. NAPC works to protect children from physical, sexual, and emotional abuse. The association was formerly known as Promise to Protect. Its website includes information about child-protection legislation.

National Center for Missing & Exploited Children (NCMEC)
Charles B. Wang International Children's Bldg., 699 Prince St.
Alexandria, VA   22314-3175
(703) 224-2150 • fax: (703) 224-2122
website: www.ncmec.org

The NCMEC's mission is to help prevent child abduction and sexual exploitation. The organization assists in finding missing children and supports victims of child abduction and sexual exploitation. Its website provides articles on sexual exploitation, sex offenders, and how to guard against online predators.

National Exchange Club Foundation (NECF)
website: http://preventchildabuse.com

The NECF provides a variety of public awareness materials designed to help inform and increase awareness of child abuse and how it can be prevented. Such projects are implemented through Exchange Clubs and Exchange Club CAP Centers across the country. It utilizes the Parent Aide program and provides support to families at risk for abuse. The NECF provides training, accreditation, technical support, guidance in agency development and management, and other supportive services to these sites.

Rape, Abuse & Incest National Network (RAINN)
2000 L St. NW, Suite 406, Washington, DC   20036
(202) 544-1034
e-mail: info@rainn.org
website: www.rainn.org

The Rape, Abuse & Incest National Network is the nation's largest sexual assault support and prevention organization. RAINN operates the National Sexual Assault Hotline at (800) 656-HOPE and carries out programs to prevent sexual assault, help victims, and ensure that rapists are brought to justice.

US Department of Justice, Criminal Division
10th & Constitution Ave. NW, Criminal Division
John C. Keeney Bldg., Suite 600, Washington, DC   20530
(202) 514-1026 • fax: (202) 514-6113
website: www.cybercrime.gov

The Computer Crime and Intellectual Property Section (CCIPS) is responsible for implementing the Justice Department's national strategies in combating computer and intellectual property crimes. CCIPS prevents, investigates, and prosecutes computer crimes by working with other government agencies, the private sector, academic institutions, and foreign counterparts. Press releases and brochures on cybercrime such as the Prosecuting Computer Crimes Manual can be accessed through the department's website.

Wired Safety
website: www.wiredsafety.org

Wired Safety is an Internet safety and help group. It provides educational material, news, assistance, and awareness on all aspects of cybercrime and abuse, privacy, security, and responsible technology use. It is also the parent group of Teen angels.org, FBI-trained teens and preteens who promote Internet safety.

Bibliography

Books

Yaman Akdeniz
Internet Child Pornography and the Law: National and International Responses. Farnham, UK: Ashgate, 2008.

George Collins and Andrew Adleman
Breaking the Cycle: Free Yourself from Sex Addiction, Porn Obsession, and Shame. Oakland, CA: New Harbinger Publications, 2011.

Council of Europe
Protecting Children from Sexual Violence: A Comprehensive Approach. Strasbourg Cedex: Council of Europe Publishing, 2010.

Charles Ess
Digital Media Ethics: Digital Media and Society. Cambridge, UK: Polity, 2009.

Stefan Fafinski
Computer Misuse: Response, Regulation and the Law. Cullompton, UK: Willan, 2009.

Timmy Fielding
Silent Victim: Growing Up in a Child Porn Ring. Bloomington, IN: iUniverse, 2012.

Alisdair Gillespie
Child Pornography: Law and Policy. London: Routledge-Cavendish, 2012.

James Michael Lampinen and Kathy Sexton-Radek
Protecting Children from Violence: Evidence-based Interventions. New York: Psychology Press, 2010.

Amanda Lenhart, Kristen Purcell, Aaron Smith, and Kathryn Zickuhr
Social Media and Young Adults. Washington, DC: Pew Internet & American Life Project, 2010.

Ian O'Donnell and Claire Milner
Child Pornography: Crime, Computers and Society. London: Willan, 2011.

Lee Rainie, Kristen Purcell, and Aaron Smith
The Social Side of the Internet. Washington, DC: Pew Internet & American Life Project, 2011.

Periodicals and Internet Sources

Associated Press
"Bishop Guilty in Child Pornography Case," *The Boston Globe*, May 5, 2011. www.boston.com.

Bryan Bender
"Pentagon Workers Tied to Child Porn," *The Boston Globe*. July 23, 2010. www.boston.com.

Katrin Bennhold
"More Arrests Likely in Pedophile Raid," *New York Times*, March 17, 2011.

Michael Bourke and Andres Hernandez
"The 'Butner Study' Redux: A Report of the Incidence of Hands-on Child Victimization by Child Pornography Offenders," *Journal of Family Violence*, 2009.

Jason Byassee
"Not Your Father's Pornography," *First Things: A Monthly Journal of Religion and Public Life*, January 2008.

The Christian Science Monitor
"'Sexting' Overreach," April 28, 2009.

Nicole Cruz | "Ingesting Poison: Adapting to Exposure to Child Pornography," *FBI Law Enforcement Bulletin*, October 2011.

Curriculum Review | "Teens Share Sexually Explicit Messages: Simple Rebellion or Dangerous Behavior?," May 2009.

Maryjoy Duncan | "The Serious Implications of 'Sexting,'" *El Chicano Weekly*, April 22, 2010.

Joshua Herman | "Sexting: It's No Joke, It's a Crime," *Illinois Bar Journal*, April 1, 2010.

Idaho State Journal | "Should Sexting Be a Crime?," April 4, 2010.

Meredith Krause | "In Harm's Way: Duty of Care for Child Exploitation and Pornography Investigators," *FBI Law Enforcement Bulletin*, January 2009.

Law & Order | "Worldwide Child Pornography Network Dismantled," January 2008.

The Mail on Sunday (London) | "Many of the Victims of Child Pornography Are Abused in Irish Homes," December 18, 2011.

Index

O

Obama, Barack, 67
O'Brian, Muireann, 68
O'Brien, Terrence, 7
Offenders. *See* Child pornography
  offenders
Oosterbaan, Drew, 64–65
Operation Flicker, 22–23
Operation Hamlet, 15
Operation Predator, 19
Oregon Forensic Institute, 70

P

Patriot Act, 44–45
Pedophilia/pedophiles, 17, 27, 69,
  76, 81
*Peer-to-Peer Networks Provide
  Ready Access to Child Pornogra-
  phy* (GAO), 29
Peer-to-peer (P2P) networks, 13,
  18–19, 28–29
People (magazine), 83
Phillips, Mike, 56, 57
Photo sharing sites, 13, 53
The Pines treatment center, 24
Popsci.com, 8
Pornography-blocking software, 71
Predator, Operation, 19
Project Flicker, 19
Project Safe Childhood, 19
Protecting Children from Internet
  Pornographers Act (2011), 37–40
Przygoda, Dan, 33–36

R

Redenius, Chad, 47–48
Robinson, Nigel, 8
Russia, 21

S

Sabra, Neal, 25
Sanchez, Julian, 40
Sensenbrenner, James, 39
Sex and Tech survey, 86
Sex Offender Treatment Program,
  73
Sexting. *See* Teen sexting
Sexual abuse
  child pornography and, 10–
    11, 14, 70
  danger of with porn, 73–74
  offenders of, 68
  police operations against, 31
  prosecution of, 69
Sexual offender registries, 34, 80,
  84–85
Shehan, John, 24
Shutterfly (online photo sharing),
  53
Social networking sites, 8, 13, 53
  See also Facebook; MySpace
Spain, 21, 68
Stop It Now organization, 7
Sweeney, Daniel J., 22
Switched (magazine), 7

T

Taboclaon, Aleah, 73–77
Teaser porn, 71
Teen sexting, 8, 84–86
Texas Department of Public
  Safety, 47
Torres, John, 21, 23
Treatment implications for por-
  nography, 76–77
Treon, Dick, 34
Trischitta, Linda, 50–54